Guitar Style

by
Joe Pass
and
Bill Thrasher

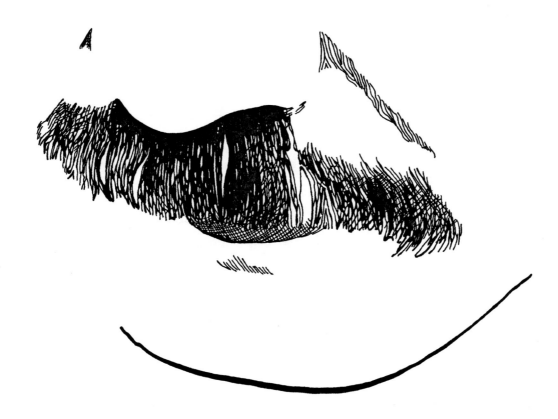

© Copyright MCMLXX Camelot - Gwyn Publishing Co.
Copyright assigned MCMLXXXV to Alfred Publishing Co., Inc.

Foreword

When we first looked at this book, it was as thick as a Bible. Yet it was immediately decided that it should be in the hands of ALL guitarists. We got together and rehashed the book that Joe and Bill spent many years on. You will find no diagrams (a cassette is available for audio-visual aid in sight-reading) and very few words. Guitar has been played by diagrams for too long which can cause players to be poor sight-readers (they read diagrams too well). There are pages which look "hard", pages which look "easy," pages that will tickle your brain. This book quickly involves the player in improvising, reading, theory, all kinds of licks, and will no doubt be considered **the** book. The enjoyment it offers while fulfilling your desires to be a fine musician is immeasurable. We hope it is the most influential force to propel you to greater playing ability. It is a study of great musical magnitude. Every note in this book is: **JOE PASS**.

The Publisher

Contents

Introduction iv

PART ONE: HARMONY 1

Chord Construction 1

Chord Embellishment 2

Chord Substitution 3

Chord Connection 5

Symmetric Chords 7

PART TWO: MELODY 11

Chord Scales 11

Altered Scales 15

Ear Training 16

Whole Tone Scales 22

Chord Resolutions 24

Improvising 32

Blues 35

Minor blues 37

Modern Blues 39

Rhythm Changes 45

3/4 Blues 50

Solo 55

Biographies 59

Introduction

Classical guitarists have had a few hundred years in which to evolve an organized, disciplined approach to playing: a ''proper'' method. The plectrum guitar, like jazz, is a product of this century, and the electric guitar is so recent an innovation that we're only beginning to recognize its possibilities as a legitimate instrument.

The early guitar players combined elements of the classic style with banjo or mandolin picking techniques to form a sort of guitar method. When I started learning to play, the instrument books available were very limiting.

Some thirty years later, when I began to have the time and inclination to teach a few students, I was shocked to discover that the situation had improved only slightly. With a couple of worthy exceptions, there was virtually nothing in existing guitar literature designed for the working musician, teacher, or even for the ''middling'' guitarist.

Experience is unquestionably the best teacher, but it should not be the serious student's only access to new knowledge. This slim volume is the first in a series of attempts to bridge the current gap between what is known and what is in print about playing guitar.

Music is an enormous subject, and no one can claim to know everything about it. Bill and I have spent, between us, about seventy years as working guitar players, and we're still learning. Our goal in this book, and in those to follow, is simply to share with you what we've managed to learn thus far.

The emphasis here is on improvisation, which seems the most neglected and widely misunderstood area of modern music, and on the ear training essential to mastery of that gentle art.

The chapters on chords, theory and harmony have been condensed from an original manuscript which was several hundred pages in length. These subjects will be treated in greater detail in subsequent volumes, as will the elements of technique, style, solo development, chord-melody solos, and much more about improvising.

No book can substitute for your own experience...there are too many things you can learn on a stand that cannot be translated into printed words. If this book provides a few new ideas, a different approach or a fresh viewpoint towards your playing, then it is a beginning...a good first step in what is hopefully the right direction.

May it please you.

Joe Pass

PART ONE: HARMONY

Intelligent improvising depends on a working understanding of the relationship between chords and melodic lines. The purpose of this section is to provide the necessary harmonic foundation for the solos in Part Two.

The chordal theory is presented in its briefest form, as it directly relates to the guitar. If some of the explanations differ from those in "formal" theory books, you're free to change the words to suit your own way of thinking. It is the idea that's important, not its explanation.

This material is designed more as a reference than a method. If these ideas are TOTALLY new to you, there may be other books you might investigate before finishing this one.

CHORD CONSTRUCTION

The C Major/Minor Scale

MAJOR CHORDS: add chord NAME to basic triad

major	1	3	5 (basic triad)	C	C	E	G			
major 6th	1	3	5 and 6	C6	C	E	G	A		
major 7th	1	3	5 and ma7	Cma7	C	E	G	B		
added 9th	1	3	5 and 9	Cadd9	C	E	G	D		
major 9th	1	3	5 and ma7 and 9	Cma9	C	E	G	B	D
6th/9th	1	3	5 and 6 and 9	C6/9	C	E	G	A	D

SEVENTH CHORDS: add chord name to a 7th (or 9th) chord

7th	1	3	5	7		C7	C	E	G	B♭
9th	1	3	5	7 and 9		C9	C	E	G	B♭ D
11th *	1	3	5	7	(9) and 11	C11	C	E	G	B♭ (D) F
13th **	1	3	5	7	(9) and 13	C13	C	E	G	B♭ (D) A

* in most guitar inversions, the 3rd is omitted from 11th chords. The 9th is often omitted from both 11th and 13th chords.

** in theory, a 13th chord also contains the 11th, but that tone is normally omitted in guitar fingerings.

MINOR CHORDS: add chord name to basic triad

minor	1	mi3	5 (basic triad)	Cm	C	E♭	G	
minor 6th	1	mi3	5 and 6	Cm6	C	E♭	G	A
minor (ma7th)	1	mi3	5 and ma7	Cm+7	C	E♭	G	B

MINOR SEVENTH CHORDS: add chord name to a m7th chord

minor 7th	1	mi3	5	7	Cm7	C	E♭	G	B♭
minor 9th	1	mi3	5	7 and 9	Cm9	C	E♭	G	B♭ D
minor 11th	1	mi3	5	7 and 11	Cm11	C	E♭	G	B♭ F

DIMINISHED SEVENTH chords are built by flatting all but the root of a 7th chord.

C7		1	3	5	7		C	E	G	Bb
* C°		1	b3	b5	6 (b7)		C	Eb	Gb	A (Bbb)

* may be written: Cdim, Cdim7, C7dim, C°, C°7, C7°

The word "AUGMENTED" in a chord name normally applies to the sharped (augmented) 5th chord tone. **

C+, Caug	1	3	#5		C	E	G#	
C+7, C7+, C7aug	1	3	#5	7	C	E	G#	Bb

** EXCEPTION: the AUGMENTED ELEVENTH chord is a regular 11th chord, but the 11th is sharped.

C+11	1	3	(5)	7	(9)	#11	C	E	(G)	Bb	(D)	F#

ALTERED CHORDS (sharp or flat 5th or 9th): just do as instructed.

C7+5-9	1	3	#5	7	b9		C	E	G#	Bb	Db	
C13-5-9	1	3	b5	7	b9	13	C	E	Gb	Bb	Db	A

"SHORTCUT" CHORD SYMBOLS

Cma7	C△7
Cma9	C△9
Cm7	C-7
Cm7-5	Cø

CHORD EMBELLISHMENT

MAJOR CHORDS: add 6, ma7, 9 and (in blues) 7. To C major chord add the notes A, B, D or (blues) Bb. For C major, play:

SEVENTH CHORDS: add 9, 13 or use 11 in sets: 11 to 7, 11 to 9, 11 to 13. To C7 add the notes D, A, or F. For C7, play:

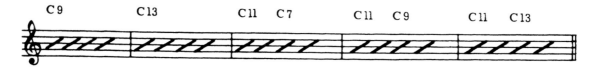

MINOR CHORDS: add 6, 7, ma7, 9 or 11. To Cm add the notes A, Bb, B, D or F. For Cm, play:

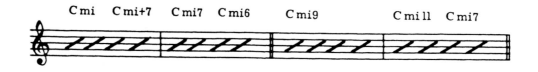

2

ALTERED CHORDS: the 5th may be sharped or flatted in any chord.
the 9th may be sharped or flatted in 7th chords.

This sequence:

may be played:

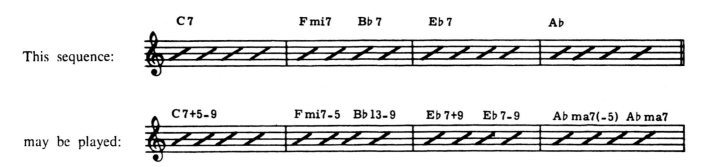

Reduce all chords to their basic form:

Cma7, C6, Cma9, C6/9   reduce to C MAJOR
C9, C11, C13−9, C9−5   reduce to C SEVENTH
Cm7, Cm9, Cm11, Cm7−5   reduce to C MINOR

CHORD SUBSTITUTION

MAJOR CHORDS: Substitute RELATIVE MINOR or SECONDARY RELATIVE MINOR
chords. For C use Am or Em

Optional:

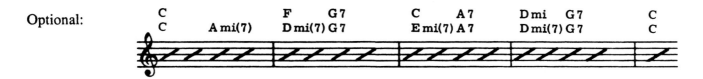

MINOR CHORDS: Substitute RELATIVE MAJOR. For Am use C

This:
becomes:

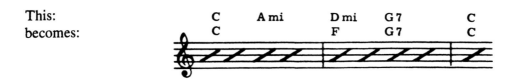

SEVENTH CHORDS: Substitute DOMINANT MINOR. For C7 use Gm

This:
becomes:

This rule may sometimes be reversed, as shown below:

This:
becomes:

3

ALL CHORDS: Substitute any chord which has as its root the FLAT FIFTH of the original chord. For C use Gb. The type of chord used (major, minor, seventh) depends upon the desired harmony. A few examples:

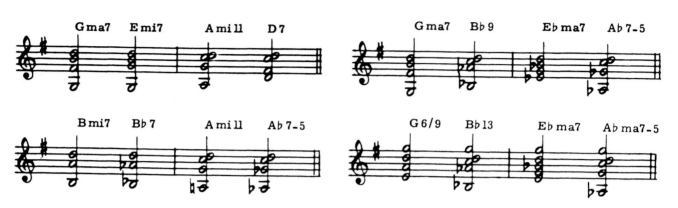

In places where the melody indicates no STRONG preference for chord type (as in the last two "turnaround" measures of a song where no melody exists), seventh chords may replace minors. Each of the following examples could be played in place of C Am Dm G7:

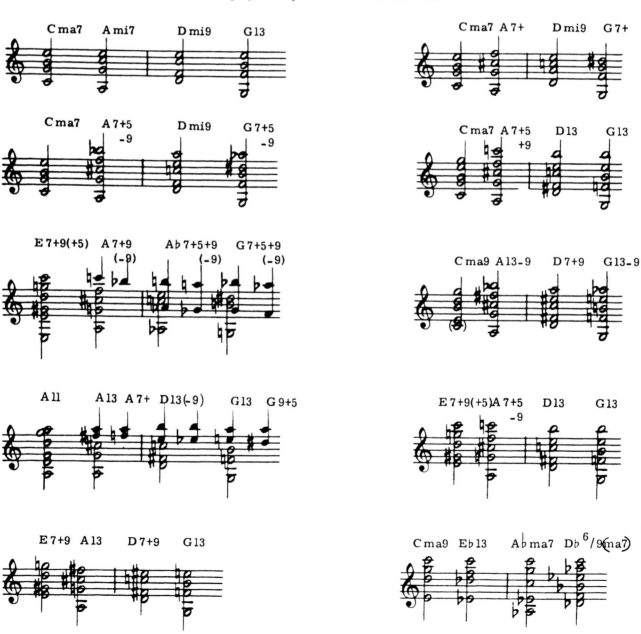

SUBSTITUTE PATTERNS

The following patterns substitute for C major. There are many possible variations, so experiment.

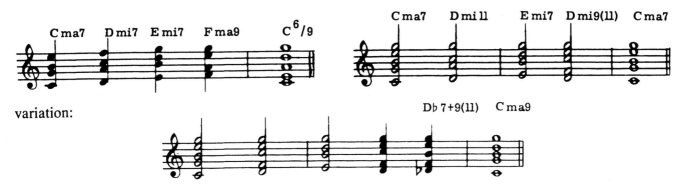

variation:

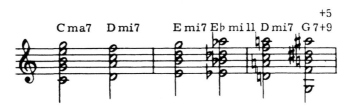

If C is moving toward G7, use this, or variations on it:

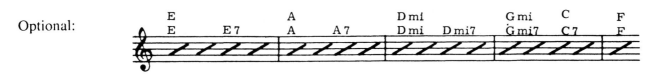

CHORD CONNECTION

SEVENTHS connect dominants, as shown below:

Optional:

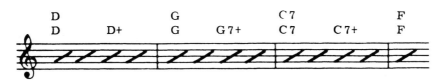

AUGMENTED chords also connect dominants:

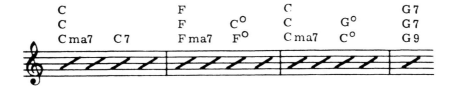

DIMINISHED chords connect subdominants. Use the diminished chord with the SAME NAME as (1) the chord being entered or (2) the chord being left:

DIMINISHED chords also connect chromatically:

5

MINOR chords connect the subdominant chord to the tonic chord:

ALL chords may be connected by moving into the chord from a half-step (one fret) above or below:

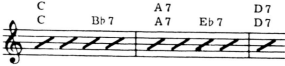

Here is a blues to illustrate the half-step (one fret) connection principle. The whole thing can be played using this one fingering:

Use other fingerings if you like. Try Am7 or A7+5±9 in the 9th measure.

These are more than just one-fret "slurs". The "pickup" chord is D7+5+9, moving down to G13 and G9 in the 1st measure. The final chord in that measure is G7+5±9 or Db13/Db9. Analyze these chords:

BACK-CYCLING

Another way to add harmonic interest to a chord pattern is to "back-cycle" through the order of dominants (cycle of fifths). This should illustrate:

C			C7	F

variations:

C			Gmi C7	F

C		Ami D7	Gmi7 C7	Fma7

Cma7	E7	Ami7 D9	Gmi7 C9	F^6/9

C^6/9	Bmi7-5 E7+9	Ami7 D7-9	Gmi9 C13-9	Fma9

Cma9 C^6/9	Bmi7-5 B♭7-5	Ami11 A♭7-5	Gmi11 G♭7-5	Fma7

NOTE: The principles of chord embellishment, substitution and connection are THEORETICALLY applicable to any given chord pattern. You'll find that some of them work nearly all the time, and some others less frequently. Try to use them in songs, and LISTEN! Your ear will tell you when it's right.

SYMMETRIC (CHROMATIC) CHORDS

Most chords can be moved up or down the fingerboard in almost any interval (half-steps, whole-steps, major or minor thirds) PROVIDED that the final chord in the symmetric sequence resolves properly into the following chord.

This study uses a single fingering throughout:

Analyze the chords below. The top four tones in each are identical. Depending upon the bass-line used, the study above could be played against C7, Gm, Gb7 or Em chords.

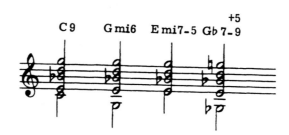

If that study were played against a C7 chord, the bass-line could move symmetrically with the chords, or just pedal a "C" note:

For the same chord (C7−5) the Gb bass note could move up with the chords, or be sustained as a pedal tone in the rhythm section:

"DIMINISHED" CHORDS

You know that a Diminished 7th chord moves up or down the fingerboard in minor third intervals. The same is true of ANY chord which has a "diminished" character (7−9, 7−5, 13−9, 7+5−9, etc.)

C7−5−9 up and down in minor thirds:

The "C7" chord in the study above could resolve into an F chord at any of the "C7" points, or from either of the "Gb7" points. The "Eb7" and "A7" chords would not resolve well into F.

You needn't limit the symmetric motion to minor thirds. In the next study, F7−9 moves quite a lot before resolving into Bb7−9:

Add appropriate bass-notes to hear the true chord sound.

The next study is basically B7 to E7 to A7 to D7:

In symmetric harmony, the chords move from one "good" point to another. What takes place between those points is up to your ear.

F13 up in minor thirds:

Try the same thing with F13−9:

F7+5+9 or B13 down in minor thirds. Resolve F7 into B♭, B13 into E:

Dm7 to G7 to C:

This fits Fm6   to A♭m6   to E♭ma7   Reduce: Fm/A♭m to E♭
         Fm6   to B♭11−9   to E♭ma7   Fm/B♭   to E♭
         Dm7−5   to G7+5±9   to Cm9   Dm/G7   to Cm

Track 7
Fm7/Bb7 to Eb   or   Dm7/G7 to Cm:

Dm7/G7 to C:

D7 to G:

Ab7 to Db:

Track 8
This study uses an Ebm triad moving symmetrically down in minor thirds. It could fit Ebm, C7, Gb7, Cm or Ab7 chords.

C7−5−9 down in minor thirds:

re-phrased:

variation:

These are just a few ideas, to help illustrate the point. The guitar is built a certain way, and lends itself to this kind of chordal thinking. Experiment until you get the feel of it. Your ear will tell you when it's right.

10

PART TWO: MELODY

Good improvising is humming or singing a melody in your mind while simultaneously playing that melody on the guitar. The sound must be in your ear and in your hand.

One of the goals of this part of the book is to provide you with some basic skills in coordinating the ear/hand relationship. More importantly, the studies and solos are designed to acquaint your ear with more MODERN sounds than are normally included in guitar books. You may have to do a lot of thinking and listening, but with a little effort you can force your ear into new harmonic ground faster than the normal process of on-the-job experience would take you there.

Every study should be transposed to all keys, and played in all possible fingerings and positions on the fingerboard. Studies which cover a range of one octave should be extended to two-octave or three-octave figurations, etc. Work them into your own music, improvise only after learning the patterns. Think in terms of SOUNDS always.

CHORD SCALES Track 9

Scale of G major:

Altered to fit G7 chord:

Chord scales are formed by altering the root scale to conform to the SIGNIFICANT chord tones. When playing against a G7 chord, the G major scale is altered to include the 7th (F), rather than the ma7th (F♯). The chord scale of G7−5 would be altered to include the flat 5th (D♭).

The G7 chord scale contains no sharps or flats. It is equivalent to the scale of C major. Within certain limitations, the C major scale fits the sound of all the following chords:

Analyze each measure carefully. It will become apparent that the scale of C major does not ALWAYS apply to every chord shown in the example. A breakdown follows:

First measure fits C, C6, Cma7, Cma9, C 6/9

Second measure fits Dm, Dm7, Dm6, Dm9, Dm11. These sounds apply to any "Dm" chord going to G7 and C.

Third measure fits Em7 when used as Secondary Relative Minor substitute for C. If the chord were Em6 or Em9 the scale would include F♯ and C♯ (D major scale.)

Fourth measure fits any F chord (F6, Fma7) used as a substitute for Dm. For a true "F major" sound, the scale would include B♭ (F major scale).

Fifth measure fits G7, G9, G11, G13. All the unaltered "G7" chords going into C major.

Sixth measure fits Am, Am7, Am9 when used as substitutes for C. For Am6 the scale would include F♯ (G major scale).

Seventh measure fits Bm7−5 going into E7(+5−9) and Am. For this chord, use (a) the Am natural minor scale (same as C major scale) or (b) the Am harmonic minor scale.

Am harmonic minor scale fits these chords:

Combining the minor scales produces results like this:

Minor chord scales may resolve into major chords:

Cm   harmonic minor scale   C   major scale

The reverse of that is often (but not always) true. Dm9 and G13, for example, each contain the MAJOR 3rd of C. While those chords may be resolved into a Cm chord, the line will imply a stronger minor sound if they include the MINOR 3rd (E♭). That is, G7+5 to Cm is a more minor-sounding resolution than G13 to Cm.

Minor chord scales are easy to form, if you keep in mind HOW the chord is being used. Notice the different chord scales used for Am in this study:

C major (Am natural minor) scale

F major scale (Am is secondary relative minor to F)

G major scale

Am harmonic minor scale

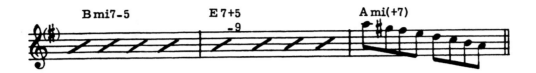

Gm harmonic minor scale

Gm natural minor (Bb major) scale

(Ascending) Cm melodic minor scale (Cm6 = Am7⁻5)

The F♮ in this last example could be played as F♯, to sound like the major 3rd of D7 and the major 7th of G.

This study illustrates the implied chord-sounds in the C major scale. The scale, played from "C" to "C", sounds like C, Cma7, C6. Played from "D" to "D" it sounds like Dm, Dm6, Dm7, etc.

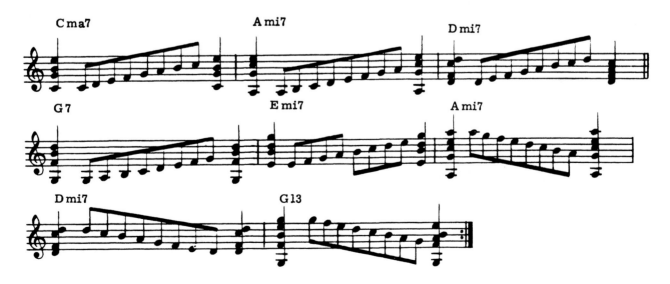

Below is a standard chord progression, showing the proper chord scales.

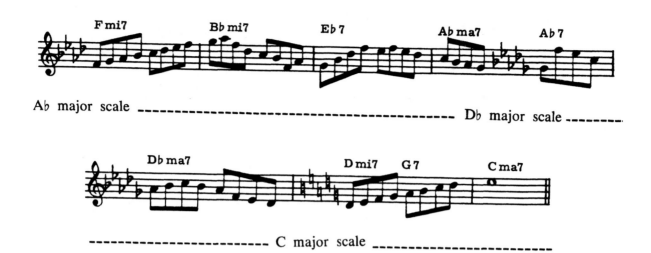

In the first measure above, the Fm7 chord could also be played using D♮ instead of D♭. (Scale of E♭ major).

Another example. In this study, the A7 chord in the 6th measure could be played using the Dm harmonic minor scale. That sounds more like A7+5−9:

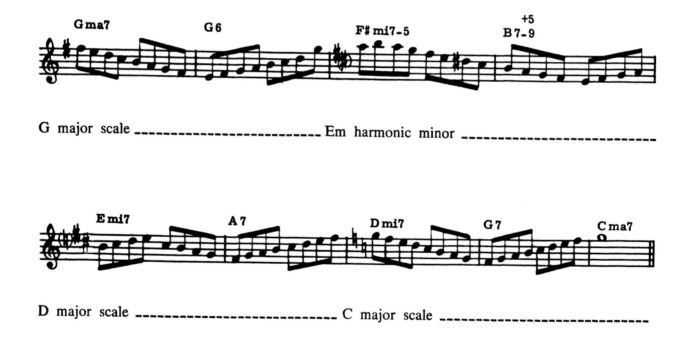

NOTE: Thinking in terms of "equivalent" scales is fine for study purposes, while your ear is learning to "hear" chord scale sounds. When improvising, you should be aware of the chords as separate entities because (as later studies will show) there are certain sounds that might fit one kind of chord (seventh) but not all others (major or minor).

The practical value of these equivalents is that while you may be THINKING of G7, for example, your left hand works in the familiar habit patterns of the C major scale.

ALTERED SCALES Track 11

In the same way that chords can be altered (+5, −5, +9, −9 etc.) the chord scales may also be altered to include those sounds. The following studies move from a "pure" G7 scale to some more modern sounds.

G7 without leaving the chord

This uses both F♯ and F♮ to heighten the "seventh" feeling:

Here the sharp 5th (D♯) is added:

G7 with passing tones (±5, ±9, ma7)

G7−5

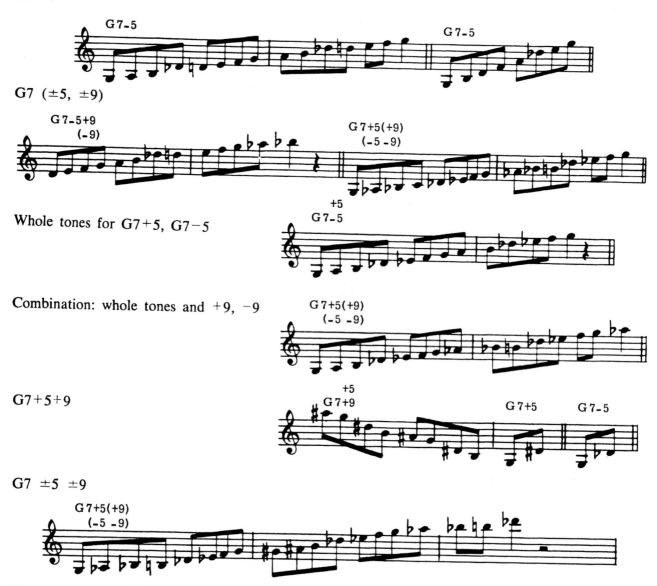

G7 (±5, ±9)

Whole tones for G7+5, G7−5

Combination: whole tones and +9, −9

G7+5+9

G7 ±5 ±9

Keep your thinking simple on these. Each study has a certain sound of its own, but they are all basically G7 sounds. Think G7.

If some of these sound a little strange, go ahead to the Ear Training studies, come back and try these later.

EAR TRAINING

Most scale studies tend to take the ear away from the basic chord sound. In the following example, only the C major scale is used, but it SOUNDS as if the chords were moving from C to Dm7, Em7, F, etc.

That same scale pattern may be played this way:

It isn't necessary to play the notes exactly as they appear above. Just try to keep hearing the chord root, C.

Another good study for ear training (and developing chord scales) is this one:

Use B♭ in that last measure and play C9. Then play up to E♭ and play C7⁺9, and so on.

A variation on the same idea:

Minor scales may be practiced in the same way, but there are three kinds of minor scales. Their differences involve the 6th and 7th scale tones:

NATURAL minor scale (Cm)

HARMONIC minor scale (Cm)

MELODIC minor scale (Cm)

In the following studies, the 6th and 7th scale tones may be played as flats or naturals. The notes which can be played both ways are marked with a "natural" sign in parenthesis (♮):

Each line shows a chord, its scale and arpeggio. Recommended practice sequence: chord, scale, chord, arpeggio, chord. Transpose to all keys, fingerings and positions.

MAJOR CHORDS:

SCALE   CHORD   ARPEGGIO

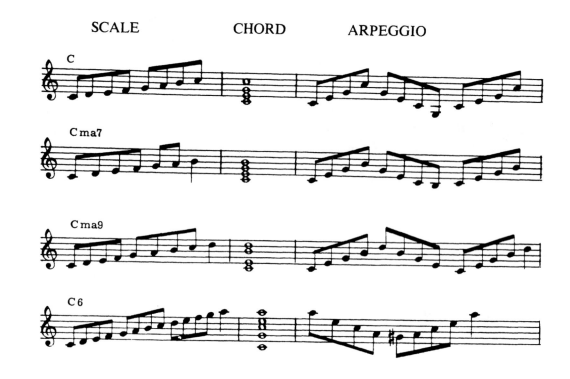

SEVENTH CHORDS:

use Db°
for C7-9

There are many variations possible in altered 7th chord scales. A few examples are shown below. Don't spend too much time on these until you've finished the more basic chord scales and arpeggios.

This sounds more modern than the "pure" C7−5 scale above. This includes the sharp and flat 5th and 9th:

Even more modern sounding. End on different chords for variety:

MINOR CHORDS:

Notes preceded by a "natural" sign in parenthesis (♮) may be played as ♭ or ♮. Try all combinations.

SCALE   CHORD   ARPEGGIO

Cm7−5 normally progresses to F7 and B♭ or B♭m. Use the natural minor scale (same as D♭ major) or the harmonic minor scale. Experiment with the optional scale tones marked below:

When in doubt about the variations in altered minor scales, think of where the chords are progressing. Below are three versions of a Cm7−5 chord scale (note key signatures):

Line 1 uses the B♭m harmonic minor scale. Line 2 uses the natural minor scale (same as D♭ major). In each of these two lines, the F7 chord might be played as F7+5−9.

Line 3 uses the B♭ major scale, but G is flatted to conform to the chord sound. The F7 chord might be played as F13−9.

In the following study, line 1 uses B♭ natural minor scale, moving into F7+5±9 and B♭m.

The "D" note in line 2 may be played as D♭ (B♭ harmonic minor scale) or as D♮, going into F7 and B♭ major.

Start and end these studies on different notes or beats for variety. Here are five variations on the same phrase:

WHOLE TONE SCALES Track 14

Whole tone scales may be played over any #5 or b5 chord. Analyze the "C" whole tone scale below:

That scale fits C7+5, C7−5, C+ or C9±5 chords. When the #9 and b9 are used in combinations with whole tone passages, they fit ALL the "C7" chords: C7+5−9, C13−5−9, C7+5+9, etc.

C7+5+9

Combinations: C7±5±9 $\qquad$ C $^{7+5+9}_{(-5-9)}$

The next four examples fit G+, G7+5, G7−5 or basically any "G7" chord:

Whole tones move chromatically through dominant passages:

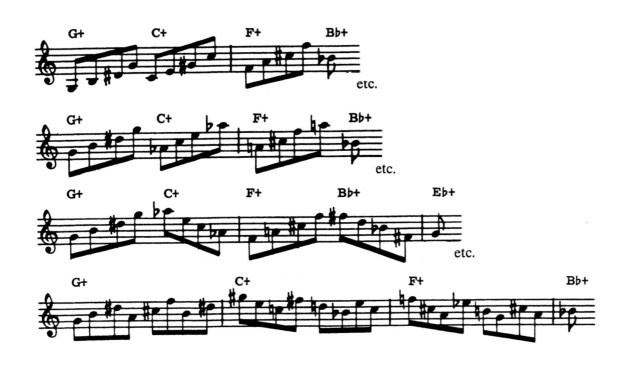

WHOLE TONE BLUES

Improvise some whole tone combinations in the blank measures, above.

CHORD RESOLUTIONS Track 16

Here are four studies showing the resolution of G7 into C (or C7). Line 4 can go to Cm if the last note is changed to Eb. Lines 1 and 3 could also stay in G7. Try to play the chords with the melody, to help your ear.

G7 to Cm7/F7

"LEAD-IN" NOTES Track 17

In the transition from one chord scale to another, there is a "lead-in" note which signals the point of departure from the preceding chord, and implies the sound of the chord to follow.

In each of these examples, the "lead-in" is the first note in the second measure:

See what you can do by changing one or two notes:

G7 to Gb

G7 to Db

G7 to Bb7

Flat B, E and A in the first measure (above) for Fm7 to Bb7

G7 to Bb7 (End on different chord tones for Bb7−9, etc.)

G7 to Bb7 (Try using Bb, Eb, Ab in the first measure for Fm7 to Bb7)

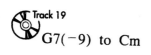

G7(−9) to Cm

This same phrase appears in the 3rd and 4th measures, below:

D7 to G

G to E7

Extend these into longer lines. The last example (above) begins this next extension:

The same (or similar) phrase may be repeated through the chord changes:

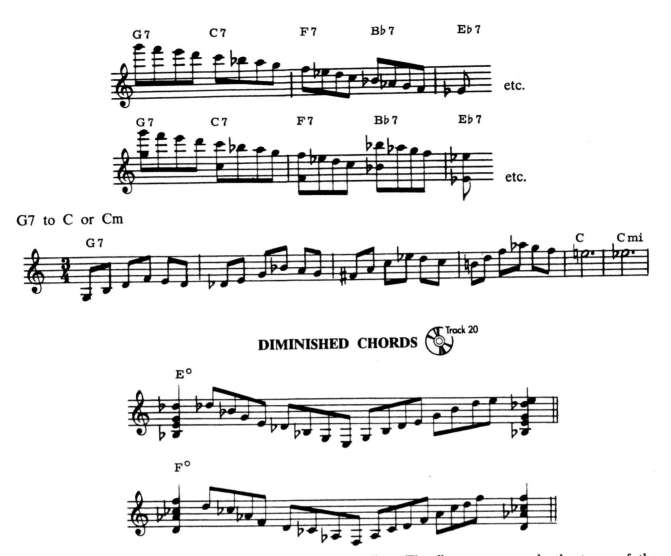

G7 to C or Cm

DIMINISHED CHORDS Track 20

Here are five practice patterns, ascending and descending. The first two use only the tones of the diminished seventh chord. The last three involve "slurs" into those tones from a half-step away:

DIMINISHED SUBSTITUTES

Notice the similarity between G7−9 and A♭°. Every 7−9 chord is (with root omitted) equivalent to a diminished chord one half-step higher. That is, diminished-sounding scales may be applied to 7−9 chords, and vice-versa.

Below is a common chord pattern, using 7−9 substitutes for the diminished chord. Note use of ♯5 in those chords.

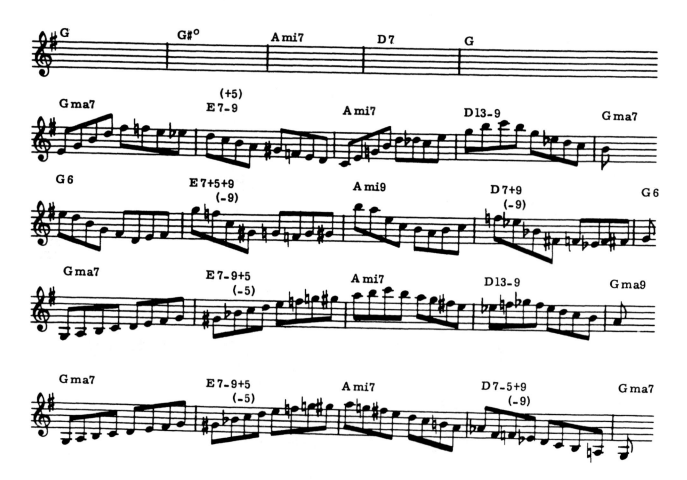

Three more variations on the same pattern (G to G♯° to Am7 to D7). Note the use of A7+9 for Am7:

Some 16th-note variations on the first two measures:

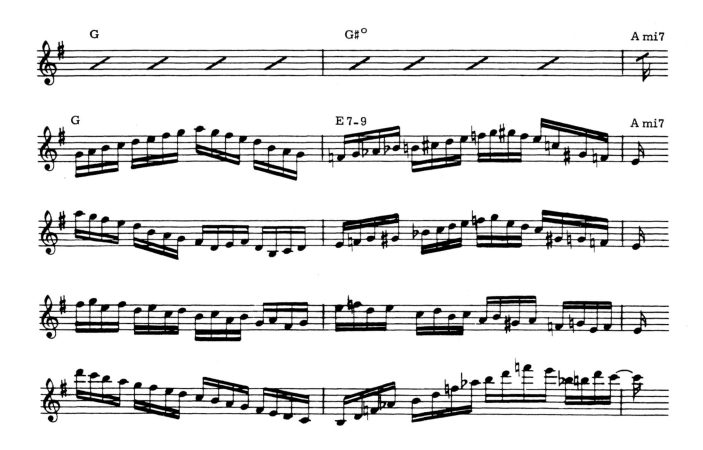

In this study, E7 becomes Bm7-5/E7-9. This gets pretty far away from the original "diminished" sound, but may be used with discretion:

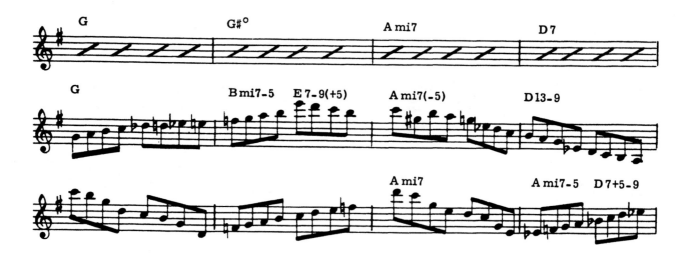

CHORDAL THINKING  Track 21

The chord shown above is Cm7-5. It is also Ebm6 or Ab9 with root omitted.

When playing a line against that chord you can THINK in Cm:

or think in Ab: (note key signature)

or in Ebm:

Depending upon where the chord is progressing, you can THINK in terms of what is most familiar to you. Resolve Cm7-5 to F7-9/Bbm. Resolve Ab9 to Db, and Ebm6 to Ab7/Db.

Here is a line "translated" from thinking in G to thinking in Db. In this particular example, thinking in Db results in fewer accidentals, but that should not be your ONLY consideration. Think in terms of LOGICAL chord sequences: G7−5 to C, Db7−5 to Gb.

Some G7 lines. These fit G7+, G7−5, G7+5−9, etc. "Translate" each from G to Db.

Extend this chord scale:

to this:

Two more examples. Try to play a chord with the melody, to help your ear, and resolve into an appropriate chord: G to C, Db to Gb.

31

IMPROVISING

One way to develop improvisational skills is to take any common chord pattern and isolate it for study. Each of the following studies shows a chord pattern in the top line. Below it are some improvisations which fit the pattern.

When you've finished these, write out any chord sequence that seems to you a "common" pattern; then improvise.

33

The next study fits the pattern: G to Em to Am to D7 (one bar each). No chord symbols appear because you are to make your own analysis.

BLUES

These solos are in straight 8th-notes. By eliminating rhythmic variety, you force the ear into building better melodies. 8th-note studies also tend to avoid the practice of playing memorized licks.

Chord symbols are for your analysis, not necessarily for accompaniment.

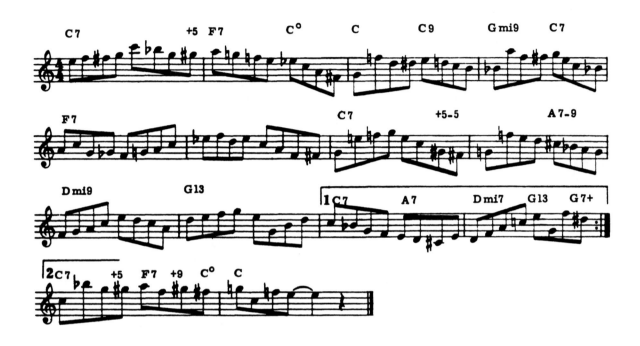

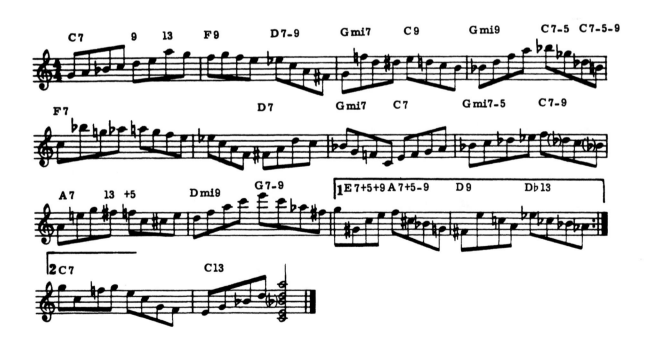

35

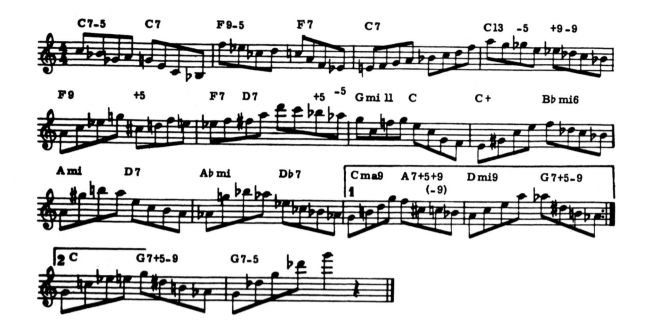

This one is in 16th-notes. It gives you more to play on each chord:

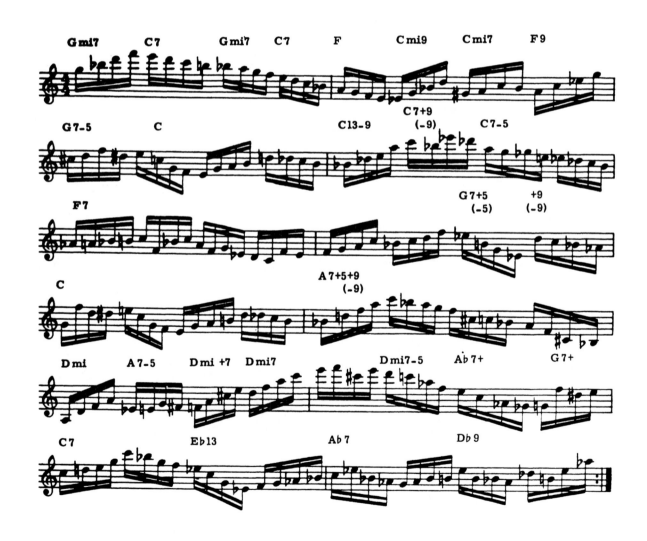

MINOR BLUES

Chord symbols are for analysis, not accompaniment:

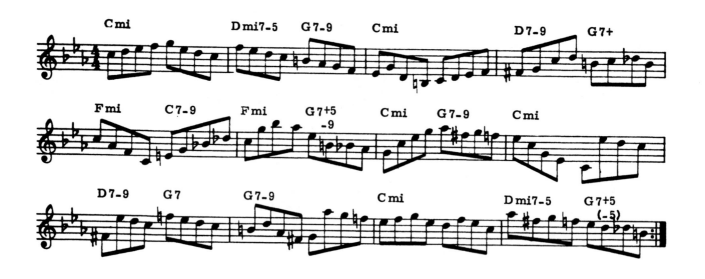

MODERN BLUES

The chords shown below represent one version of blues changes.

There are many possible variations. The chord symbols in the studies are to help your analysis of the melodic lines, but they'll give an approximation of the proper accompaniment.

These are designed to be played consecutively, so the final measure in each chorus may contain the "pickups" for the following chorus.

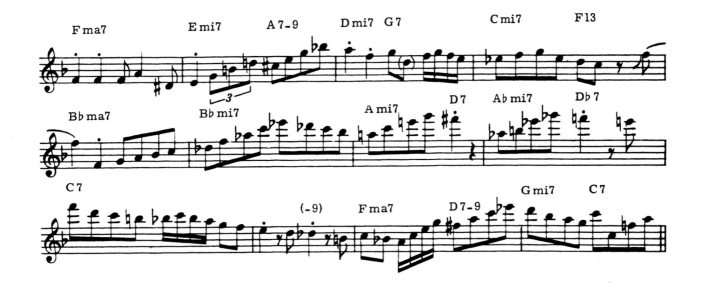

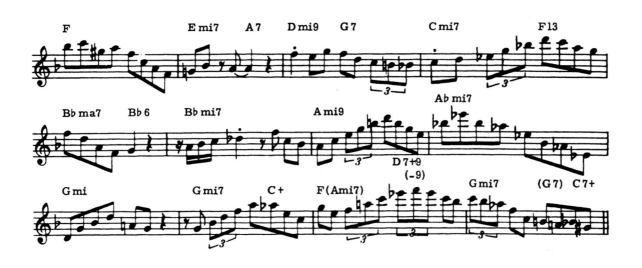

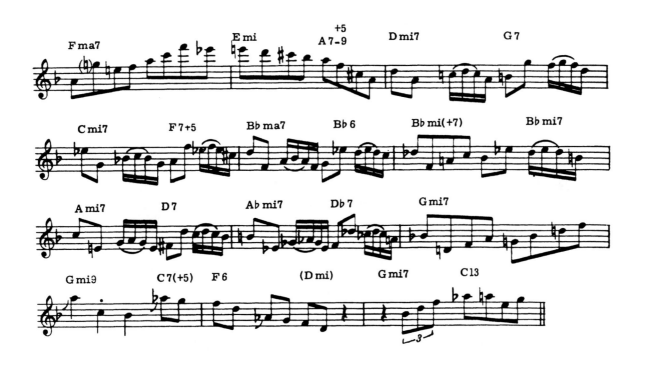

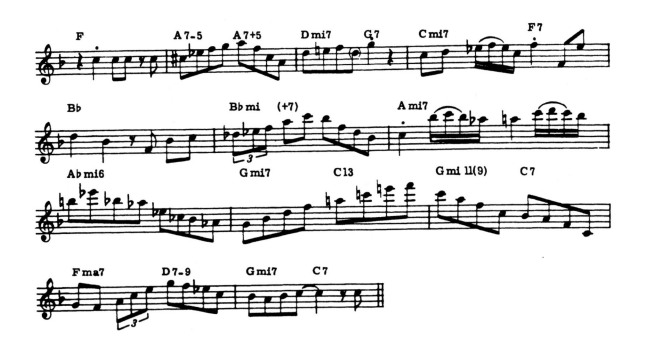

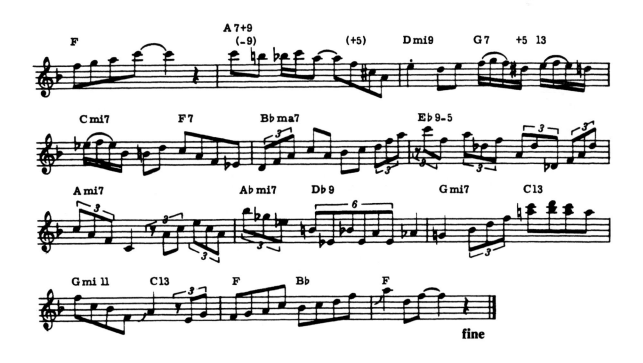

fine

43

Improvise in the blank measures:

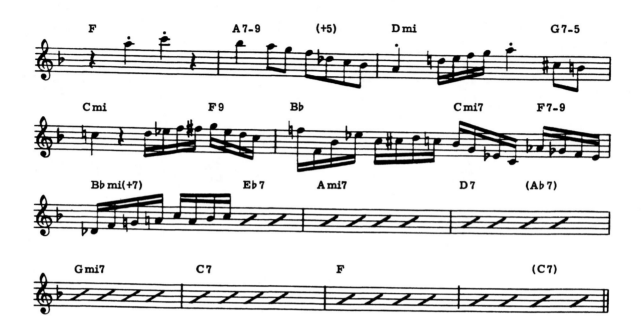

Modern blues are also played against this chord pattern. Use chord embellishment, substitution, etc.

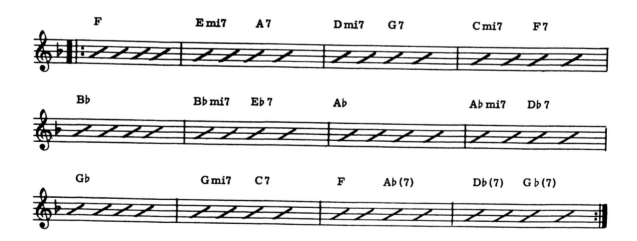

44

RHYTHM CHANGES

Rhythm changes are normally played at very fast tempos, so the chord patterns vary, depending on the player. The chart shows two BASIC "rhythm" patterns:

Track 24

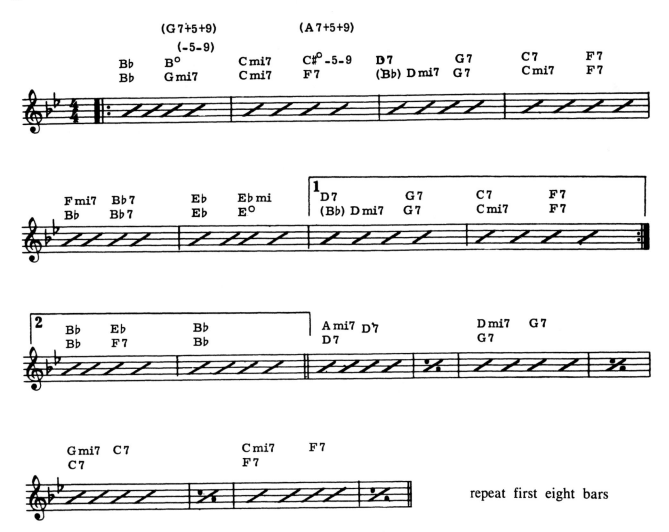

As usual, the chord symbols in each chorus represent the harmonic THINKING in the melody line.

Notice the bridge (starting at bar 17) consists of a single two-bar phrase, repeated through the chords:

Track 25

47

48

The chords in the unmarked measures are just standard "rhythm" changes. The phrase which begins in bar 8 is re-stated during the next few bars. Don't over-analyze this: just play it and LISTEN.

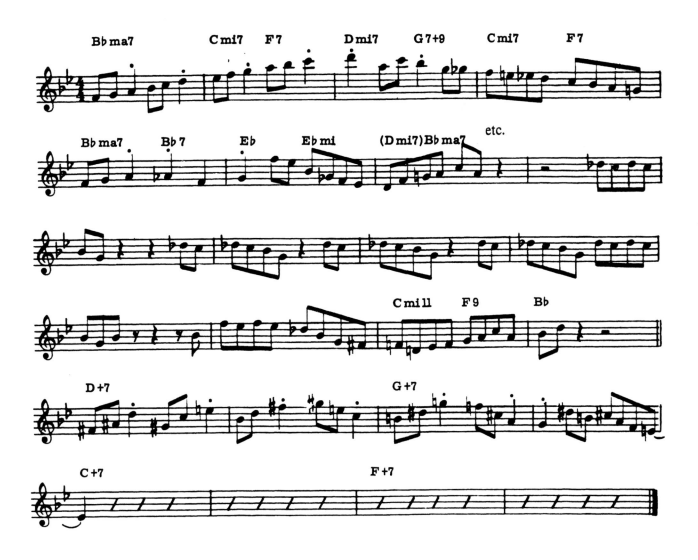

Finish the chorus with something of your own. Below are two examples of two-bar phrases which can be repeated through a line of dominant 7th chords. Try them on the bridge, above.

3/4 BLUES

This is another set of blues changes, in 3/4 time.

 Track 26

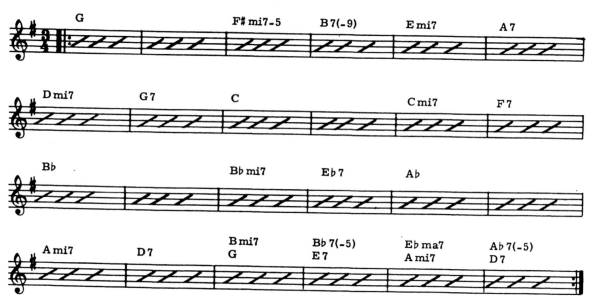

The solos are designed to be played consecutively, so the last bar in each chorus may contain the "pickups" to the ensuing chorus.

 Track 27

INTRO:

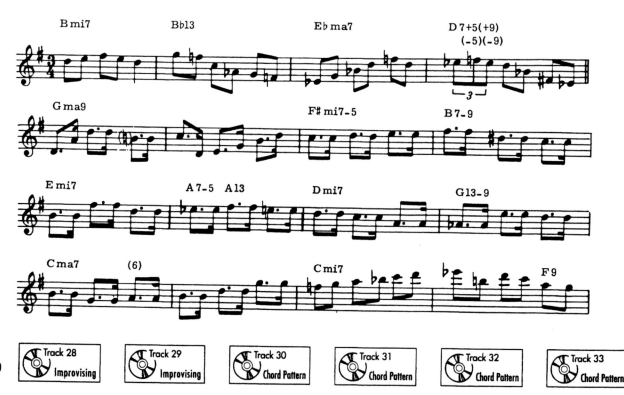

Track 28 Improvising | Track 29 Improvising | Track 30 Chord Pattern | Track 31 Chord Pattern | Track 32 Chord Pattern | Track 33 Chord Pattern

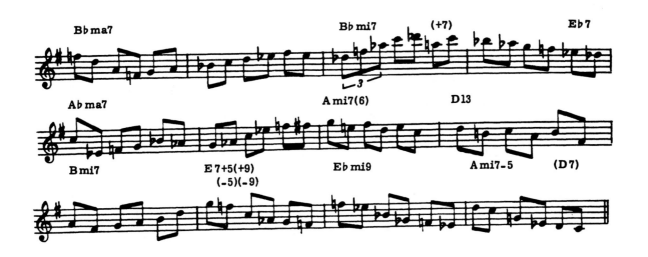

Solo as Recorded by Joe Pass on Pacific Jazz PJ-85 album "For Django".

This chart shows some of the basic chordal thinking used in the solo. With chord embellishment and substitution, variations are almost limitless. No chord symbols are indicated throughout the solo, so you must do your own analysis.

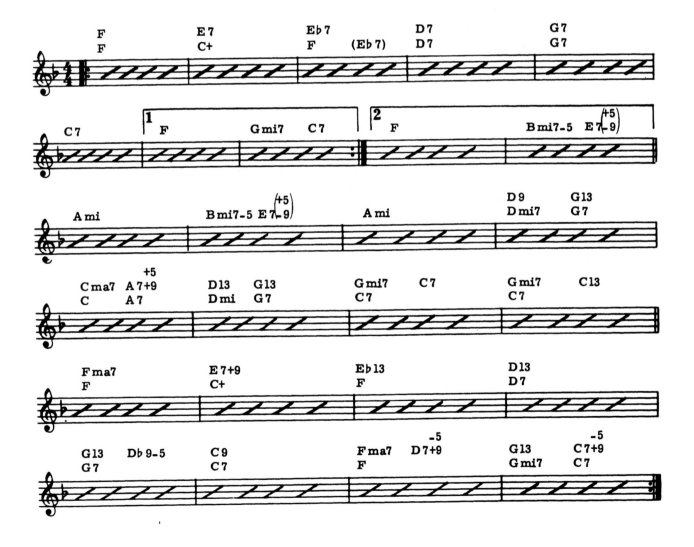

56

57

Biographies

Born Joseph Anthony Passalaqua (one of 5 children) in New Brunswick, New Jersey, Joe grew up in a steel mill town. He began playing the guitar at the age of 9. To help support his family, he started playing professionally at 14. He practiced 6 hours a day. Being an avid fan of Django Reinhardt, it was natural that he first played in "Hot Club of France" type groups. Listening to Django probably helped form his ear training for the beautiful melodic lines he creates. He plays no "trick" licks—every note means something. Because of this, Joe is one of the few guitarists who is admired by all instrumentalists. His work was later influenced by Charlie Parker, Dizzy Gillespie, Coleman Hawkins, and others. In 1963, his fame grew as leader of "Sounds of Synanon Tour" and he won Down Beat's New Star Award. Joe was virtually discovered by Leonard Feather (author of ENCYCLOPEDIA OF JAZZ) and recorded many fine albums—CATCH ME, 12-STRING GUITAR, FOR DJANGO, SIMPLICITY, SIGN OF THE TIMES, STONE JAZZ. He was featured on BRASSAMBA, FOLD 'N FLUTE (with Bud Shank), MOMENT OF TRUTH, PORTRAITS, ON STAGE (with Gerald Wilson), and SOMETHIN' SPECIAL, ON TIME, OUT FRONT, JAZZ AS I FEEL IT (with Les McCann). He has also been a sideman with George Shearing, Louie Bellson, Groove Holmes, Carmel Jones, Frank Sinatra, Julie London, Della Reese, Johnny Mathis, Leslie Uggams and many others. Joe has appeared regularly on such TV shows as: JAZZ SCENE USA, THE STEVE ALLEN SHOW, THE WOODY WOODBURY SHOW, THE JOHNNY CARSON SHOW, THE GEORGE SHEARING SHOW, as well as his own personal appearances.

Joe Pass

Bill Thrasher, who lives in Santa Barbara, spent much tedious time writing and correlating this book with Joe. He is a successful teacher, guitarist, illustrator and an all-around intellectual artist. These two have been good friends for a long time and got together to write this book which will be of invaluable help to all musicians. Bill's work proves him to be an extremely talented "great."

Joe is currently doing studio work, personal concerts and teaching. He resides in Van Nuys, California. Joe's music reflects honest beauty and rock-solid authority which comes from years of practicing and professional experience, not to mention that special ingredient: MUSICAL GENIUS. In these pages you will find much evidence of one of the world's great guitarists.

Bill Thrasher